Early American People

Sarah Howarth

SIMON & SCHUSTER
YOUNG BOOKS

For Joanna

First published in Great Britain in 1994 by

Simon & Schuster Young Books
Campus 400
Maylands Avenue
Hemel Hempstead
Hertfordshire HP2 7EZ

Designed by Neil Adams
Illustrations by Philip McNeill

Text copyright © 1994 by Sarah Howarth
Illustrations copyright © 1994 by Philip McNeill

Typeset by DP Press Ltd, Sevenoaks, Kent

Printed and bound by Proost International Book Co., Belgium

A CIP record for this book can be obtained from the British Library

ISBN 07500 1525 X

Picture acknowledgments

Picture research by Donna Thynne

The publishers would like to thank the following for their permission to reproduce copyright material:
The Bettmann Archive, New York: pp 22, 31, 43; The Bridgeman Art Library: pp 6, 11; Brooklyn Museum, Brooklyn, New York/Dick S Ramsay Fund: p 27 (from "American Painting" Weidenfeld and Nicolson); Bruce Coleman Inc, USA: p 28; E.T. Archive: pp 10, 33; The Gibbes Museum of Art/Carolina Art Association: p 30 "View of Mulberry Plantation (House and Street)" by Thomas Coram, oil on paper; Harvard University Portrait Collection, Harvard University Art Museums: pp 14 (given by Robert Winthrop representing the Winthrop family, in 1964 to Harvard University), 24 (gift of Mrs Frank M. Clark, 1940); The Hulton Deutsch Collection: pp 29, 41; Library of Congress, Washington D.C.: p 21; The Linnean Society/Eileen Tweedy: p 35; The Mansell Collection: pp 13, 34, 36; Massachusetts Historical Society: p 16 (from "American Painting" Weidenfeld and Nicolson); National Portrait Gallery, London: p 38; Peter Newark/Western Americana: pp 8, 12, 32, 40, 45; New York Historical Society: pp 9, 15; New York Public Library: pp 3, 5, 7, 39, 44; Pennsylvania Academy of Fine Arts, Philadelphia: p 19 (from "American Painting" Weidenfeld and Nicolson); Yale University Art Gallery: p 17 (gift of Robert Sherman White, B.A. 1899, LL.B 1902); The Colonial Williamsburg Foundation: pp 18 (Abby Aldrich Rockefeller Folk Art Center), 20, 23, 42.

CONTENTS

INTRODUCTION

Imagine that you had to tell someone from another planet about the world in which we live today. How would you do it? One way would be to think of different sorts of people and the work that they do. Who would you choose to give a really good picture of everyday life? You might pick people who grow the food we eat; people who work in factories, making the things that we buy in shops; people who help others, like nurses and teachers; people who take command of our world, such as politicians and soldiers. Without these people, life in the twentieth century would be completely different.

This book will tell you about people who lived at another time in history: those who lived in North America between the sixteenth century and the eighteenth century. This was a time when the first Europeans settled in North America, making contact with the Native Americans and shaping a new way of life. The story of the British colonies in New England was especially dramatic, as close ties with Europe were replaced by a growing sense of independence. In the chapters that follow, you can find out about the different sorts of people who lived at this time, and how the work that they did created the world in which they lived.

THE NEWCOMER

The newcomers who stepped ashore in America in search of a new way of life came from all sorts of backgrounds. This vivid description comes from a history of the settlers' early years in America, written by a famous preacher named Cotton Mather (1663–1728):

'Many worthy persons transplanted themselves and their families to New England: gentlemen of ancient families, ministers of the Gospel, merchants, farmers and craftsmen.'

Land of opportunities

To the people of the 1600s and 1700s, America seemed to be a land of opportunities. It seemed to have something to offer to almost everyone; it did not matter how

A settlement in the colony of Pennsylvania. Compare the buildings here with the picture of the Native American village on the next page. Are the shelters built in the same way?

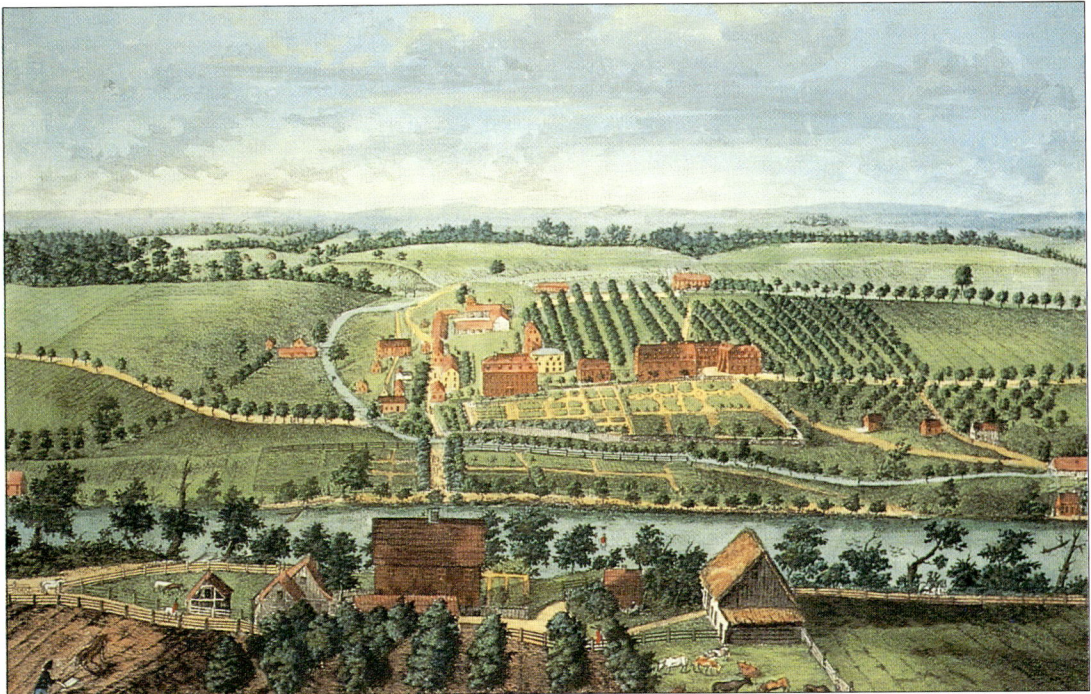

rich or poor they were, or what their religious beliefs were, or what country they came from. For country people who owned no land, America offered the chance to have a farm of their own. For merchants, the country promised good trading. Dutch newcomers who set up the colony of 'New Netherland' were particularly keen traders, for example. For craftsmen who found it difficult to set up shop in Europe, America held the prospect of settlers eager to buy their goods. French Protestant craftsmen were among those who seized this opportunity. For many people who suffered persecution at home because of their religious beliefs – including the French Protestants – America provided the chance to worship God freely. And for governments which wanted to rid their country of people held in prison, America seemed the ideal place to send them. Sweden was one country which sent a number of convicts (prisoners) to its American colony of 'New Sweden'.

One newcomer to America, the Englishman John White, painted a series of watercolours showing the Native Americans of Virginia and their way of life. Here he shows a Native American settlement of the 1580s.

Roots of freedom

Perhaps the most important 'something' America had to offer was a great deal of freedom. Settlers there had plenty of opportunity to build a way of life which suited them. This personal freedom is something that people in the Western world take for granted today. Its roots lie back in the times of the first American settlers.

Founding the colonies

The story of how different colonies were founded gives us an insight into the aims and background of different newcomers to America. Virginia, New England, Maryland and Pennsylvania are good examples.

Virginia was the first permanent British colony to be set up. It developed from a settler community founded at Jamestown in 1607. The hope of prosperity was an important aim for many of the people who lived there.

The words of a contemporary ballad give us a clue about this. *'Day wages for the labourer, and for his great content, a house and garden plot he'll have,'* promised the song. For many poor people who lived in Europe, this would have seemed like heaven-sent riches.

The next British colonies to be founded tell a story of newcomers with very different aims. These were the colonies of New England. They were founded by people of great religious conviction: Protestant Christians, who wanted their religion to shape every part of daily life. Their opinions were unpopular, even forbidden, in many parts of Europe. Among the colonies set up by Protestants were Plymouth, Massachusetts Bay, Connecticut and New Haven.

Religion played an important part in the founding of other colonies too. Maryland was planned as a place where Roman Catholic newcomers would be allowed to worship without interference. Pennsylvania provided a refuge for a group of Christians called Quakers.

Beginning the world anew

One especially important tie bound all the newcomers together, no matter who they were: they were building a new life together. There was everything to be done, from growing food to exploring the land. The words of John Winthrop, first governor of Massachusetts (1588–1649), tell us a great deal about early life in an unknown land:

'The governor and a group of men went up river. They named the first brook Beaver Brook because beavers had cut down great trees there. Another place they called Cheese Rock, for when they went to eat, they had only cheese.'

In these early days of exploring, naming and building, a new feeling of identity was growing. Before long the new settlers would no longer think of themselves as Europeans, but as Americans.

A corner of New York in the seventeenth century. Keeping livestock was important to the newcomers. Animals provided food, haulage and transport.

THE NATIVE AMERICAN

T he newcomers were not the first people to live in America. Here an early settler named Francis Higginson (1587–1630) records his first impressions of the natives for whom America was already home:

'They are a tall and strong-limbed people. They go naked save only they are in part covered with beasts' skins.'

The inhabitants of America

A Native American warrior with pipe and tattoos. The Native Americans soon became caught up in quarrels between different groups of European settlers, such as the French and English.

The area between the Atlantic coast and the Mississippi River, which was the first area of North America settled by Europeans, was home to four main language groups of Native Americans: the Siouan, the Muskhogean, the Iroquois and the Algonquian. Other tribes of Native Americans lived on the central plains of America, in the north-west and in the south-west, although few Europeans met them at this time. These groups lived in communities called tribes, under the leadership of a chief. There were about 500,000 Native Americans living in North America late in the fifteenth century when the European expedition led by Christopher Columbus (*c*. 1445–1506) arrived.

Age-old customs

The Native Americans followed age-old traditions. Those described here are the ways of the groups who lived along the

east coast. For men, this meant hunting and fishing for food, and fighting battles with neighbouring tribes. For women, it meant cooking on an open fire, caring for children, making simple clothes from animal skins and, in some places, growing food crops.

The tools and techniques used by the Native Americans were also very ancient. They relied on whatever the land provided for food, although many groups, such as the Algonquin people, also farmed the land. These people adapted the landscape to their needs, growing crops like maize, beans and squash (marrow). They made their weapons and tools from bone, animal skin, stone and wood. For hunting and fighting they used home-made snares, bows, arrows with bone or stone tips, tomahawks and spears.

Religious beliefs too had their origins in the depths of time. While beliefs varied, the Native Americans generally worshipped a 'Great Spirit', the sun, moon and other powers. As in many other ancient religions, magical beliefs were linked with religious ideas. 'Medicine men', or shamans, combined the two elements. They were believed to have power over evil spirits because they had a special relationship with the spirit world. It was thought that this power enabled them to cure illnesses.

At home

Many Native Americans lived in villages. Some tribes built long huts in their villages, with a number of families living in each hut. This was the custom among the Iroquois people. Other tribes built tents out of animal skins in their villages. From time to time the Native Americans would move on. *'They change their home from place to place,'* wrote one European settler.

A Native American chief, painted by a settler in the 1580s. Native American skills helped many of the first European settlers to survive in America. Farming and cooking techniques were especially important.

Scenes of Native American village life have been handed down across the years in the paintings of an Englishman named John White. White visited North America in the late 1580s. His pictures give us many images of men, women and children, village shelters, corn fields, fishing, cooking, eating and other activities. His paintings are an important source of evidence, helping us find out about the Native Americans. So too are accounts written by European settlers and explorers. The words of one explorer, Captain James Smith, like John White's paintings, tell us about the everyday life of the Native Americans of Virginia. *'Their houses are built of young trees bowed over and tied, and covered with mats or the bark of trees. They are very warm,'* he wrote.

In some places the Native American way of life left a spectacular mark on the landscape. Here, for example, you can see the 'Great Serpent' Mound in Ohio. Dug from the earth, the mound is about 0.4 kilometres long and takes the shape of a serpent. It is thought that this was a special religious site.

Who tells the story?

There is a very important reason why we use pictures and descriptions by European settlers to learn about the Native Americans. This is because the Native Americans did not write things down. To record great events, they passed information on by word of mouth, or they made special 'wampum belts' – belts studded with elaborate patterns of beads which carried a meaning.

When the Europeans first arrived in America, their relationship with the Native Americans was often friendly. *'We found the people most loving and faithful,'* wrote one settler. But the two sides were soon at war. Many settlers let fear and hatred affect their view of the Native Americans when they put pen to paper. We have to remember that there were few people to tell the other side of the story.

THE GOVERNOR

A typical day at work for one of the newcomers' leaders was described by a man who lived at the time:

'The governor sent a message to the members of the assembly. He ordered them to come to the council chamber. Here he directed them to choose an officer.'

Powers and people

When the countries of Europe came to set up colonies (foreign lands that they conquered and controlled), there was always one very important question to be answered. How were the colonies to be ruled? Arrangements were slightly different in each colony, but the most usual way was to select one man as the governor, or leader, of the colony.

In parts of America controlled by France, the governor was chosen by the French king. This happened in Canada, for example. The governor of Canada was always given very detailed orders by the king, so that he knew exactly what he could and could

This is the earliest picture of New Amsterdam – a town that was later renamed New York. Dutch traders established a fort here in the 1620s. Traders and settlers at New Amsterdam were ruled by a trading company.

not do. In the colonies set up by Britain, governors were not treated quite like this. The king and government in Britain found that they could rarely spare the time to send detailed instructions to America, and governors of the British colonies became used to making many of their own decisions. In many colonies, such as New Hampshire and the Carolinas, the governor was chosen by the British king. In some other colonies, called the 'proprietary' colonies, the governor was chosen by the 'proprietor' (owner) of the colony. But the proprietor did not have complete freedom, because his choice had to be approved by the king. This custom was practised in the proprietary colonies of Maryland and Pennsylvania. In some colonies, arrangements were made for the governor to be elected by a special group of voters.

Busy days

The governor had so many duties that it was often difficult to snatch a few minutes away from work. John Winthrop, governor of Massachusetts, described his busy days in a letter. *'I am so over-pressed with business as I have no time for mine own private occasions,'* he explained.

It was the governor's job to see that the law was obeyed and to defend the colony. He had to consult with the men who represented the wishes of the settlers at great councils called assemblies. Special officials were appointed to help the governor in his work.

Rebels and heroes

The governor was a powerful figure. Some governors used their powers in an unpopular way. This was the story in Virginia late in the 1600s, where the governor, Sir William Berkeley, lost much popularity. In 1676 a rebellion against him broke out. It was led by a man named Nathaniel Bacon, and became known as Bacon's Rebellion.

John Winthrop, governor of Massachusetts. Winthrop did not believe that everyone should have a voice in questions of politics. This sort of view was very common in Europe at this time. But in America, opinions like this began to be overturned.

But disagreement on this scale between the governor and the people of his colony was unusual. The work of many governors was respected by the people they ruled. Some leaders even went down in the folk traditions of the colony – such as Captain John Smith (1579–1631), who served as president of Virginia. Captain Smith became famous because of the story of his capture by the Powhatan group of Native Americans and his rescue by Pocahontas, the Powhatan chief's daughter.

The centre of town government in seventeenth-century New York. Important decisions were taken within these walls.

Bright hopes for the future

People left Europe for the New World of America with all sorts of hopes for the future. The type of government they set up when they landed reveals a great deal about their hopes and ambitions. For some people, trade was the most important goal. These settlers sometimes organized their government rather like a trading company. Dutch people who came to the New York area in the 1620s did this. Their leader was chosen by a Dutch trading company called the West India Company. For other settlers, such as the Pilgrim Fathers of Plymouth colony in New England, the opportunity to worship God in their own way was the most important goal. In colonies like Plymouth, religious ideas played an important part in government.

THE GOODWIFE

'**G**oodwife' was a name given to married women in early America. The records of a law court in Connecticut in the 1600s introduce us to two goodwives:

'The court commands that the Bible that was sent to Goodwife Williams should be delivered now to Goodwife Harrison.'

What's in a name?

Names were very important to people who lived at this time, because they carried all sorts of messages about how rich or important someone was. 'Goodwife' was a name like this. 'Goodwife' meant more than 'Mrs' does today. It not only meant that a woman was married, but that she was a member of a particular social group. It was often used for women who were married to craftsmen or small farmers, for instance. The name 'goodwife' carried another message too. It meant a woman who was a respected, law-abiding member of the community.

A face from the days of the early settlers. This picture of a lady called Anne Pollard was painted in 1721.

Names and status

Many different titles were used at this time. 'Goodman' meant an honest man of middling wealth. Titles like 'gentleman', 'esquire' or 'master' were kept for the wealthiest and most important men in the British colonies, such as the planters (land-owners) of the south. Poorer people had no special titles. They were known just by their surnames, or by their Christian names – for example, as Robinson or James.

To be given a special title was a sign that someone

was doing well in the world. But the title could be taken away if a person became unpopular with his or her neighbours. Records from Massachusetts describe how this happened to a man named Josias Plastowe in 1631. Josias had stolen corn from Native Americans who lived near his home. As a punishment, the court declared that he was *'to be called by the name of Josias, and not Mr Plastowe as formerly he used to be'*. Stories like this show how important titles were to people at the time.

Goodwives, hard lives

But although they were sometimes given special titles, pioneering women settlers such as the 'goodwives' of New England had to work extremely hard. A picture of their life is given by William Bradford (1590–1657), governor of Plymouth colony. He tells us about their duties in the home, preparing meals, looking after the children and *'washing cloaths'*. Women also had an important part to play in helping to support the colony and to make it self-sufficient in food. Bradford tells us about this as well: *'The women went willingly to the field to get corn, taking their little ones with them.'* Women in many of the first colonies spent their days like this.

In the American colonies, life for many women was freer than it was in Europe. But complete freedom was unheard of. Women were expected to listen to their husbands and fathers, like the gentleman shown here.

Working women

Women from other social backgrounds had work to do too. In the new towns of America, some women had the opportunity to go into business, usually working side by side with their husbands. Some ran printers' shops, published newspapers, set up millinery (hat-making), dress-making and grocery stores, or ran inns and coffee-houses. We get a glimpse of one woman who went into business in the writing of a famous American named Benjamin Franklin (1706–1790). Franklin described a woman who ran a printing business in the town of Charleston, South Carolina. She *'managed the*

Women carried out many tasks in the home and on the farm. This picture shows a homestead and its inhabitants. It gives us a glimpse of some of the work that was done day by day.

business with great success and was able to buy the printing house for her son,' Franklin wrote. In Europe at this time it was unusual for women to work like this. They were expected to fill their time with unpaid household tasks. However, in America there was a small but growing number of new opportunities for women.

On the plantation

The wives and daughters of wealthy planters had duties on their estates. They helped to deliver babies and looked after slaves who fell sick. Some took an interest in farming, like Eliza Lucas Pinckney, who helped to introduce the indigo plant (which yields a purple dye) to mainland America in the 1740s.

THE APPRENTICE

Work began at an early age for children in the 1600s and 1700s. In many American towns, children went to serve as apprentices to working craftsmen. One man from Connecticut recorded:

'My will is that my son, Gregory, be put an apprentice to a godly man for the space of five years.'

A training for life

The story of Gregory the apprentice was not at all unusual. Many children, boys and girls alike, trained for work in this way. Lodging with their master, they learned the skills of his trade. Training began at about the age of 10, and lasted for up to nine years. The arrangement was carefully planned in advance. The master provided food, clothes and lodging for the apprentice. In return he got free help in his business.

The apprentice was given a thorough training. People at this time rarely changed their jobs, so apprenticeship was looked on as providing a training for life. Many different sorts of skills were handed on in this way. Goldsmiths, printers, carpenters, blacksmiths and tailors, for instance, all took on apprentices. So too did doctors and apothecaries (people who prepared and sold medicines), for in these times even medicine was learned on the job.

A blacksmith at work with his young apprentice. The apprentice lad is working the bellows, which was used to puff air on to the fire and keep it hot while the blacksmith worked.

The carpenter's work shop rattled and rasped to the sound of hammers and saws. Here we can see some of the tools that made the noise.

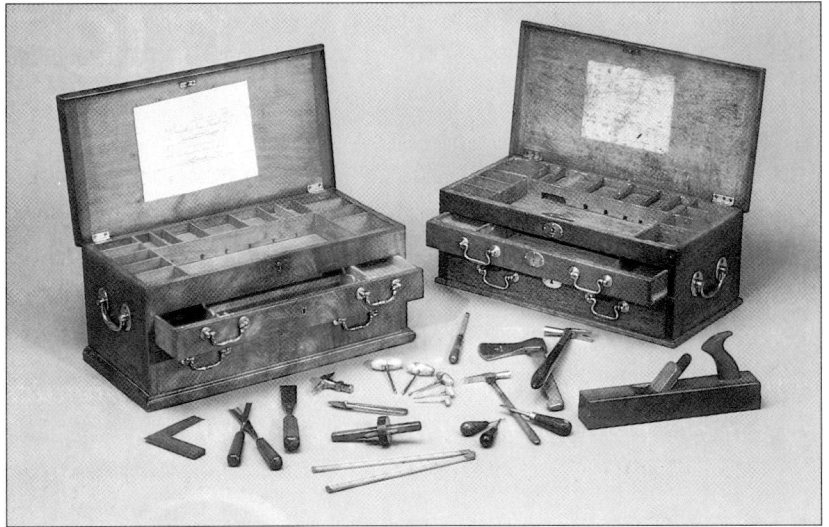

Writing it down

Arrangements to take on an apprentice were written down in a special legal document. Looking at such contracts helps us learn what an apprentice's life was like. Here is the contract drawn up for a girl who lived in the town of Boston, Massachusetts, in the 1630s. What does it tell us?

'Lucy Smith is bound as an apprentice to Mr Roger Ludlow for seven years. He is to find her meat, drink and clothes. At the end of her time he is to give her the sum of five pounds.'

Starting adult life

It was not just apprentices who had work to do. Even children who were not sent away from home as apprentices were expected to be useful. Country families were always glad of an extra pair of hands, and there were always tasks waiting for farmers' children. Helping to plant corn and other crops in the fields, working at harvest time, or looking after the animals were all part of a day's work.

Girls had to help with household work as well. This meant all sorts of jobs, for most country families lived

too far from the stores in town to be able to buy what they needed. From soap to syrups to cure coughs and fevers, everything had to be made at home. Just such a scene of family life was drawn by Governor Winthrop of Massachusetts in the 1600s. *'Two little girls sat by a great heap of logs, plucking birds,'* he wrote. Plucking birds was dreary work, but at the end of it there was a turkey or a chicken ready for the pot, and a heap of feathers for pillows. By helping out in this way, children helped their families to survive.

The title page of a famous pamphlet called 'Common Sense', printed in 1776. The pamphlet was written by a man named Tom Paine who worked with a printer and wrote for a newspaper in Philadelphia. It attacked the links between the American colonies and Britain.

A question of obedience

Children were expected to carry out their parents' wishes. Choosing a trade for a young apprentice, for instance, was seen as a matter for parents to decide and children to obey. Sometimes, however, there were disagreements. When Benjamin Franklin was ordered into the family candle-making work shop at the age of 10, tempers flew:

'I worked cutting wick for the candles, attending the shop, and doing errands. I disliked the trade and had a strong inclination for the sea. My father declared against it.'

In the end, Franklin defied his father. But it was not the sea that he chose; Franklin found he had energy to try his hand at almost everything. He printed, wrote, published, learned foreign languages, set up a fire service and a public library – and invented gadgets like the lightning conductor and a portable stove.

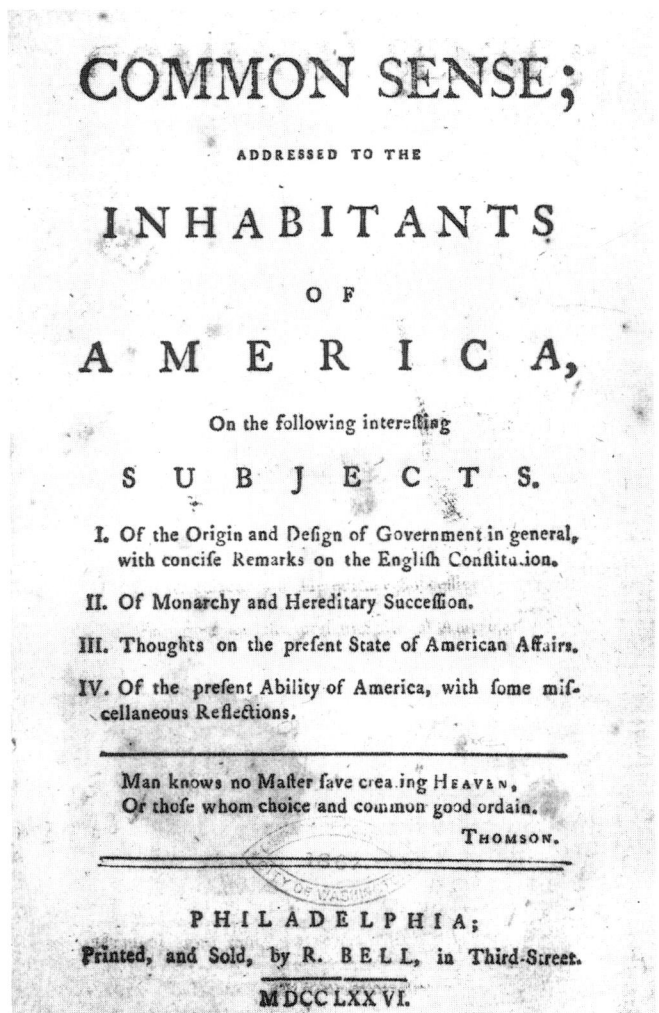

COMMON SENSE;

ADDRESSED TO THE

INHABITANTS

OF

AMERICA,

On the following interesting

SUBJECTS.

I. Of the Origin and Design of Government in general, with concise Remarks on the English Constitution.

II. Of Monarchy and Hereditary Succession.

III. Thoughts on the present State of American Affairs.

IV. Of the present Ability of America, with some miscellaneous Reflections.

Man knows no Master save creating HEAVEN,
Or those whom choice and common good ordain.
THOMSON.

PHILADELPHIA;
Printed, and Sold, by R. BELL, in Third-Street.
MDCCLXXVI.

THE PURITAN

The word 'Puritan' was first used as a nickname. It described Christians with strict Protestant beliefs. These are the words of a man, named Richard Baxter, who lived in the seventeenth century:

'For reading Scripture when others were dancing on the Lord's Day [Sunday], *for praying and for correcting drunkards and swearers, my father was named a Puritan.'*

The beginnings

Puritanism was born at a time of great religious change during the 1500s and 1600s. This change was called the Reformation, a movement that challenged the practices and some of the beliefs of the Catholic church. This led to the setting up of Protestant churches which in some countries, such as England, were supported by the state. Fired by the ideas of thinkers like John Calvin (1509–1564), some Protestants, known as Puritans, did not think the changes went far enough. They wanted to

The seal (special stamp for documents) of the first colony at Massachusetts. The words above the picture come from the Bible. Many Puritans settled in colonies like Massachusetts during the seventeenth century. The Bible provided them with their rules for living.

'purify' the Protestant religion and model it on the example of the first Christian church. The Bible was at the heart of their faith. Puritans were prepared to disobey anyone – king, queen or church leader – if they believed that they were being asked to act in a way that was contrary to the Bible.

Proud to be different

Puritan beliefs were unpopular with many people. When Richard Baxter's neighbours called someone a Puritan, it was not meant as a compliment; it was an insult. The story was the same in many other places. In some countries, Puritan beliefs were forbidden. *'I will make them conform* [fit in] *or I will drive them out of the land – or do worse,'* threatened one European king. Yet the Puritans were proud to be different. They refused to give up their beliefs, despite persecution.

Like a city on a hill

In 1620 a group of Protestants who wanted to leave the Church of England sailed from Britain to America, where they founded Plymouth colony. They were known as the 'Pilgrim Fathers'. Others, particularly

The Pilgrims pray after arriving safely in the new world.

Puritans who feared that soon they would be completely unable to worship God as they wanted, soon followed. Massachusetts Bay colony was founded by Puritans.

The Puritans who settled in America were making a bold experiment. They wanted to build a land where religion ruled every part of day-to-day life. We must *'obey the Scriptures in all things,'* said one settler. One man in particular tried to sum up the dream of the Puritan colonies: John Winthrop, governor of Massachusetts. *'We shall be as a city upon a hill,'* he declared. *'The eyes of all people are upon us.'* Winthrop expressed the Puritans' feeling that they were meant to set an example to the world by living good and religious lives.

A Puritan preacher. Puritans were unpopular in Europe, and many left to start a new life in America.

Puritan past

Religious worship was very important to the Puritan settlers. Attending the meeting house (Puritan church) to listen to long sermons, pray and hear the Bible read was the central point of community life. People who did not treat Sunday as a day of rest and worship were called 'Sabbath (Sunday) breakers'. They could be punished by law. Official documents record the fate of people who outraged public opinion in this way. *'John Baker shall be whipped for shooting birds on the Sabbath day,'* proclaimed one document. The Puritans set high standards of behaviour. Swearing, drinking, gambling, being lazy and many other personal faults were treated as crimes. These too were punished by law. In 1633 a New England settler was punished for just such a crime. He was *'ordered to stand with a white sheet of paper on his back. On it the word DRUNKARD shall be written in great letters.'*

Religious faith even played a part in politics in New England. Only men who were church members could vote for the governor and other officials, for instance. Religion also shaped the laws, introducing ideas of justice and personal rights which were radical for the time. These Puritan ideals were often remembered and honoured in later American history, but it should be remembered that the Puritans were just as intolerant of people who did not share their religious beliefs as the churches in Europe had been intolerant of Puritanism.

THE SERVANT

The first ships to sail for America brought many people who wanted to work there. They were taken on as servants:

'What shall be the employment for us there? Working in a dairy? Doing washing? What shall be the wages?'

These were the questions asked by one group of women who arrived as servants.

Signing up for service

The settlers had more work to do than hands to do it. They desperately wanted workers. Advertisements were placed in Europe to encourage people to come to work in America. One advertisement of the 1600s read:

A homestead and farm being carved out of forest ground. To the early settlers, there seemed to be plenty of land for them to take over. Many servants were given a plot of land when their serving days were over.

THE SERVANT

'Take note all craftsmen, blacksmiths, and carpenters, ship-builders, fishermen, brick-makers, weavers, shoemakers, and labouring men and women who are willing to go to Virginia and live there!'

Someone who replied to an advertisement such as this signed a special document called an indenture. This explained the terms on which he or she would work in America as a servant. The servant agreed to work for a set number of years. In return, his or her master agreed to pay for the servant to travel out to America. The master also agreed to look after the servant when he or she arrived, providing food, clothing and shelter.

Servants who made an agreement like this were known as 'indentured servants'. Many, many people who were too poor to pay to travel to America arrived as newcomers in this way. During the 1700s, about 135,000 indentured servants arrived in the middle colonies alone. They came from countries such as Scotland, Ireland, England and Germany.

Sunrise to sunset

The servants described at the beginning of this chapter wanted to know what work they would do. The answer was – anything and everything. From sunrise to sunset the settlers of early America had work to do. There was land to clear, crops to grow. There were houses to build, tools and furniture to make. Men who worked as servants often helped with tasks like these. Then there were hundreds of household tasks: cooking simple corn-based dishes like hasty pudding and succotash; cleaning; making clothes; making soap and simple medicines. Household work was seen as women's work, and women servants would help with these jobs.

Servants were also wanted for the sort of work which would be done by people working for wages today. They were taken on to keep accounts, for example, or to

work as carpenters, shop assistants, barrel-makers, barbers and printers' assistants.

In all their work, the settlers and their servants had to rely on their own labour. There were no labour-saving machines at this time. Hard work was expected from everyone. This was especially true in the colonies set up by Puritans. *'No person shall spend his time unprofitably under pain of punishment,'* thundered one of the laws made in Puritan Massachusetts. As you can see, for the Puritans, laziness was as bad as crime. The belief in hard work has been important to the people of America ever since.

Goodbye to poverty

People who came to work as servants had known hard times in Europe. Poverty, unemployment and low wages were all too common there. In America they hoped for a bright future. Servants had to work only for a few years – usually four. Then they were free to live and work as they chose. Special arrangements were made to give them a start in their new life. Often the master agreed to give the servant clothes, tools and land to live on. Customs such as these held out hope for poor people who arrived as servants. In Maryland in the 1640s, for example, it was the custom for *'every man servant to have land granted him at the end of their time of service'*. In these times when land meant wealth, many people found this a tempting offer.

In America, settlers felt that they had the opportunity to make money and grow rich. Then they could afford land, fine houses and elegant clothes. The lady shown here came from just such a wealthy background.

THE PLANTER

In the year 1713, a plantation in Barbados was advertised for sale:

'To be sold, a plantation. To include a new mansion house, sugar-stores, 180 negro slaves ...'

The words of this advertisement conjure up a picture of a wealthy planter and the land on which he grew valuable crops, such as sugar. This life-style did not develop everywhere (there were no planters around New York, for instance), but in parts of eastern North America it was very important.

Running a plantation

This house belonged to Thomas Jefferson (1743–1826), a Virginia planter, who became president of the United States. Jefferson designed the home himself.

The planter's life was spent running his plantation – a farm worked on a very large scale. Business took up much of his time. There were lands to manage, crops to check, and orders to be given to the negro slaves who did all the work. Planters grew a range of crops. In the Caribbean, most planters grew sugar-cane. Those in Maryland and Virginia devoted their energy to tobacco-growing. In the Carolinas, crops of rice and indigo were produced.

Most planters sold the crops they grew. When it was time to sell, a merchant came to call. As most plantations in the south were situated by rivers, the merchant's boat tied up at a wharf on the plantation so that tobacco and other produce could be taken on board. A planter from Virginia who lived in the eighteenth century recorded how he was visited by a ship called the *Marlbro'*: *'The Marlbro' came below the mud bank yesterday, and at once a boat came to have my tobacco.'*

Before ships like these sailed for the markets of Europe, there would be time to take orders for any

goods the planter wanted to buy. These would be bought in Europe and carried back next time the merchant called. Some planters ran into debt this way. But even so, the planters were some of the richest people in early America.

Buying slaves at an auction. Slaves were sold to the highest bidder. They were used as workers on the estates of wealthy landowners.

Masters of the land

Many planters came from extremely wealthy families. The planter who was visited by the *Marlbro'* came from just such a background. His father was nicknamed 'King' Carter because he made such a fortune out of land and tobacco. Other planters also became rich in this way. Let's look at the story of one of these men, a man named William Byrd, and see what it tells us.

William Byrd was an early settler in America. He came to Virginia in 1671 as a very young man. He set up as a tobacco-farmer and bought a plantation called Westover. Prosperity came to Westover, and Byrd had a mansion, tobacco warehouse and shop built there. Then Byrd decided to become a ship-owner. He began to trade with the West Indies, sending food, grain and other goods to be sold there. On the return journey,

sugar, slaves and rum were brought back to be sold on the mainland.

But William Byrd was not just a successful businessman and farmer. Like many other planters, he was involved in local politics. He had a place in the assembly which ruled the colony and played an important part in local decision-making. Byrd's story gives us a glimpse of the planters' way of life. Above all it shows how planters became wealthy and powerful figures, masters of the land about them.

A view of a plantation. The plantation was like a small village. Many different buildings were found there; a grand house for the planter and his family, store-houses for crops and other goods, and huts for the slaves.

Leisurely days?

Wealthy planter families such as the Byrds and the Carters had a comfortable life-style. There were servants and slaves to see to the household tasks. One writer, who lived in the 1700s, thought the planters had far too little to do. *'The gentlemen planters are above every occupation but eating, drinking, smoking and sleeping,'* he declared. In reality, many planters had more than enough to do to fill their days. Many were keenly interested in subjects such as law, medicine and science. Some put their interests to practical use – by treating their families and slaves when they fell sick, for example. *'The planter's wife takes great care of her slaves and serves as their doctor,'* recorded one document.

THE SLAVE

Not every newcomer chose life in America. Here one eighteenth-century writer, a man named Robert Beverley, tells us about some of the people who were brought there by force – African slaves:

'Slaves are the Negroes and their children. They are called slaves because they have to work their whole lives.'

A question of workers

When Beverley wrote, slavery was beginning to become very important in America. There were always too few workers for the thriving farms and businesses that the settlers hoped to run. On the plantations of southern colonies like Virginia, using slave labour seemed to be the answer.

Slavery was an accepted part of life on the plantations of British colonies such as Virginia and the Carolinas. Here you can see slaves being sold to new owners.

Journey of horror

The slave-trade grew up to supply plantations like these with a steady stream of workers. The story of that trade was one of inhuman cruelty. It began in Africa, where men, women and children were captured by African and Arab traders. After a long, exhausting march to the coast, shackled with ropes, the captives were sold to merchants from the countries of Europe – Britain, France, Spain, the Netherlands, Portugal. They were then loaded on to ships set to sail the Atlantic. On arrival in America, the slaves were sold to planters.

It was a profitable business for all the merchants concerned. To them it did not matter that conditions on board ship were appalling. It did not matter that the human cargo was so squashed together that the slaves could not stand up, nor that disease and filth turned the slaves' quarters into an area *'like a slaughter house'*, as one contemporary put it. There were fortunes to be made, and for the slave-traders of cities such as Bristol, Liverpool and Lancaster in England, that was all that counted. The slaves' loss of freedom, and the journey of horror on which thousands died, did not enter into the slave-traders' calculations.

Charlestown, July 24th, 1769.

TO BE SOLD,

On THURSDAY the third Day of AUGUST next,

A CARGO

OF

NINETY-FOUR

PRIME, HEALTHY

NEGROES,

CONSISTING OF

Thirty-nine MEN, Fifteen BOYS, Twenty-four WOMEN, and Sixteen GIRLS.

JUST ARRIVED,

In the Brigantine DEMBIA, *Francis Bare*, Master, from SIERRA-LEON, by

DAVID & JOHN DEAS.

Slave-traders made a good living by bringing slaves to America and selling them there. This poster advertises a sale of newly arrived slaves. What does it tell us about the way that traders thought about slaves?

Life in a new land

The fields of the southern colonies of North America, where tobacco, rice and indigo were grown, were the journey's end for the slaves. Robert Beverley tells us about the life that was waiting for the slaves when they arrived there: *'The slaves are employed tilling and manuring the land, sowing and planting tobacco and corn.'* Many slaves were employed in farming activities like these. Thousands more were employed on the sugar plantations of the West Indies.

The slaves' life was hard, as you can tell from the words of one wealthy planter who ran his estates with slave labour: *'Nothing is so sure to spoil your slaves than to give them little to do. That will teach them to do nothing at all!'* Opinions like these were shared by many slave-owners.

The laws of each colony set out the relationship between master and slave. There were many punishments to keep slaves in order. Slave-owners had the right to whip or even burn their slaves, for a slave was regarded as a piece of property, just like the tobacco crop or the sugar-cane in the fields. In Barbados, there was no penalty if a master kill-ed or seriously disabled a slave while beating him or her. Runaway slaves were tracked down with dogs and punished.

For the slaves who worked on a plantation, 'home' was a roughly-built compound of huts. These were usually set at some distance from the great mansion house on the plantation where the master and his family lived. In the few hours each week that were not devoted to work on the master's plantation, there was just enough time to grow a little food – and sometimes to remember the African songs and dances of the slaves' first home.

An overseer supervises slaves as they work. Slaves formed the work force on large plantations. Their owners had time to spare for all sorts of leisure activities.

Ideas of freedom

In time, the white settlers of America began to question whether it was right to use fellow human-beings as slaves. Many ideas about freedom began to take shape at the time of the War of Independence in the 1770s and 1780s.

THE FUR TRADER

In the seventeenth century, dealing in the fur trade meant money – and lots of it:

'Furs and skins, such as beavers, otters, muskrats, racoons, wild cats, elk, buffalo and many others are sold by the Indians of the country to the settlers. They sell to the merchants, who transport the furs into England and other places.'

From the back woods to Europe

This account of the fur trade was written by a man named George Alsop, who came to America as a servant in the 1650s. He was writing about the British colony of Maryland, but the story he told was true of other parts of America too. Alsop's description tells us about the long trade route from the back woods of America to the markets of Europe. It began with Native American hunters. The hunters' skills were in demand from the very first days of their contact with the European newcomers. Explorers and settlers were keen to obtain furs from animals hunted by Native Americans. In their

European merchants and Native Americans meet to trade. Fur was highly prized and the desire to trade brought the people of the Old World into contact with the people of the New World.

turn, the American tribes were eager to obtain goods from the Europeans – strange, interesting goods they had never seen before: brass kettles, cloth, sugar, buttons, looking-glasses, stockings, gunpowder, guns, brandy. The two sides were quick to make deals: American furs in exchange for European goods.

Fur was very valuable in the countries of Europe. In 1662 a famous Englishman named Samuel Pepys paid over £4 for a hat made of beaver fur. For an ordinary working family, this was the equivalent of more than a quarter of a whole year's income. Facts and figures like this show that furs commanded high prices. Beaver hats, fur linings and trimmings for coats – such items were only for the wealthy few. Merchants who had the furs of America to sell could be sure of making a good living.

Furs and finances

The fur trade rescued some of the first settlers in America from financial disaster. The Pilgrim Fathers of Plymouth colony, for example, owed money to merchants in England for the cost of their ocean-crossing and for the supplies needed in the early days to set up the colony. The sale of furs helped pay off this loan. William Bradford, governor of Plymouth colony, recorded the settlers' feelings of relief when trade went well.

For other Europeans, the fur trade was a matter of making money. As far as the French were concerned, it was one of the main reasons for exploring America. At Quebec and Montreal in the north, the French set up trading posts to tap this profitable trade. From bases such as these, young fur-trappers went out by canoe to spend the long winter months hunting with the Native Americans. On the return journey each canoe was

The ginseng plant has been used in medicine for many hundreds of years. It grew wild in North America. Merchants from Britain and other countries wanted Native Americans such as the Cherokees to provide them with ginseng. The plant could then be shipped overseas and sold.

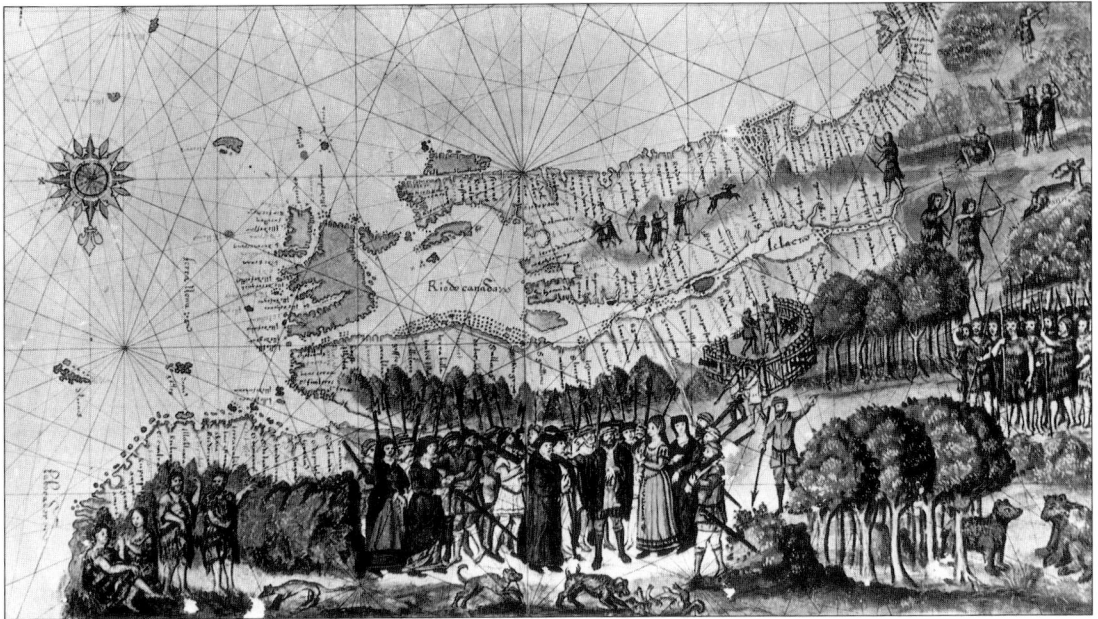

This picture shows part of the story of European world exploration during the sixteenth century; Jacques Cartier landing in Canada. Cartier explored territory which became important to the Europeans as a source of furs.

loaded with skins. Just one canoe could carry 600 beaver skins – and each skin could be sold to the merchants of Montreal for a gold dollar. The French became masters of the fur trade in this area. There was keen rivalry with the British trappers who operated to the north at Hudson's Bay and in the colonies to the south.

Exploiting and exploring the environment

The great demand for fur meant that the wildlife of America was hunted as never before. Gradually the hunters, newcomers and Native Americans alike, realized that they had killed too many animals. The supply of furs was drying up. Some colonies passed laws to restrict hunting and preserve the number of animals. Another response to the problem was simply to drive into new areas, areas that the settlers had not yet explored. The quest for furs was one reason why the settlers pushed their frontiers ever westwards. Westward expansion during the 1700s brought conflict as the French, British and Native Americans were competing for the same land.

THE CONSTABLE

A picture of the work that a constable had to do comes from records made in the courts of Connecticut in the 1600s:

'Raising the chase for murderers, peace-breakers, thieves, robbers and burglars, taking people who drink greatly, swear, break the Sabbath or tell lies.'

These things were all part of a constable's responsibilities.

Carrying out the law

Working as a constable meant taking a hand in the way that the community was governed. This was man's work, for women were not expected to be involved in public life in this way.

The constable was an important official. He was appointed by the local court and took an oath to carry out his duties faithfully. Records from the settlers' very first days in America tell us about these things: *'John Woodbury is chosen constable of Salem. He did now take the oath of constable.'* These words describe how newcomers made their first arrangements to keep law and order in New England in the 1630s. John Woodbury – and constables like him in many other towns – had to work for the court, catch criminals, collect fines, carry out punishments, deal with legal papers and see that town life was as peaceful as possible.

Punishing crime

Crime was severely punished at this time, and the constable was sometimes called on to supervise or carry out punishments. Many thieves were punished physically as well as being fined and ordered to return the goods they had stolen. *'If any person shall commit burglary, he shall be branded on the forehead with the letter "B",'* proclaimed the law. Criminals could be whipped for other offences. This happened to a servant who had been cheeky to his master, a man who stole a loaf of bread, another who sold a bottle of water pretending that it was medicine, and a boy who sold tools belonging to his master. Some criminals were punished by being set in the pillory or stocks. This punishment was planned as a way of making fun of the culprit. He would be locked by the hands or feet to a wooden post, and left there for passers-by to tease or throw things at. In Connecticut, people who drank too much could be *'set in the stocks for one hour or more in some open place as the weather permits'*.

Helping to keep law and order was part of the constable's work. Sometimes this meant seeing wrong-doers were punished – like the two men set in the stocks here.

Small settlements to busy communities

Not all the work that a constable had to do involved law and order. Constables also took part in many aspects of everyday town life. There might be taxes to collect, for example. This was a job which involved meeting many local people, from butchers and bakers to craftsmen and labourers. Sometimes the constable had to help when hogs belonging to local farmers wandered away from home. On other occasions he was expected to help draw up official records. In 1634 the constable in Boston, Massachusetts, was busy with work like this. Along with four of the most important men in town, he was ordered to make a survey of the land belonging to all the town's inhabitants. *'Houses, corn fields, mowing grounds and other lands'* were to be recorded in a book so that in future anyone could find out who owned each piece of land.

The constable worked with other people too, as he went about his duties. These included the surveyor of highways, whose job was to keep an eye on the state of local roads, and the captain of the militia, who commanded the local defence force. The number of

All sorts of buildings were going up in the thriving towns of America during the 1700s. Here is a view of the hospital and other buildings in Philadelphia.

officials needed to run the town seemed to grow all the time. The work of men like these helped the colonies develop from small groups of settlers into busy, well-run communities.

Power from the people

The way that officials such as the constable were chosen was one small part of a very big change in the way that people in America thought about power. In Europe at this time, few people except the very rich had any opportunity to influence decisions that were made on matters of law and politics. In America the settlers decided that men should have a chance to make their ideas known so long as they owned a certain amount of land or belonged to a particular local church. They did not have to come from aristocratic families. These settlers chose men to represent them in the courts and assemblies which ruled each colony. The charter (document) which set out how the colony of Maryland was to be ruled, for example, put it like this: *'You may make laws with the advice and approval of the freemen, or the majority of them, or their deputies.'* Arrangements of this kind meant that many men in the community would be able to have a say in local politics. Choosing officials like the constable was part of this process.

THE SMUGGLER

L ate in the 1700s, George Washington (1732–1799), the first president of the United States, looked back on his life. He called to mind many people who believed that smugglers were right to break the law:

'They complained that trade was crippled, and thought that smuggling was a just way to escape some of the harmful taxes.'

The smuggler's trade

Trade between Europe and the British colonies in America was governed by special laws passed by the Parliament in London, England. Trade laws placed taxes on cargoes such as tea and alcohol and directed that the tax should be paid before such goods could be bought and sold. Smugglers operated outside the law. They landed their goods illegally and avoided paying tax. Many merchants turned smuggler when times

Pirates and smugglers roamed the seas shown on this sixteenth-century map. The Caribbean was especially well known as a haunt of pirates.

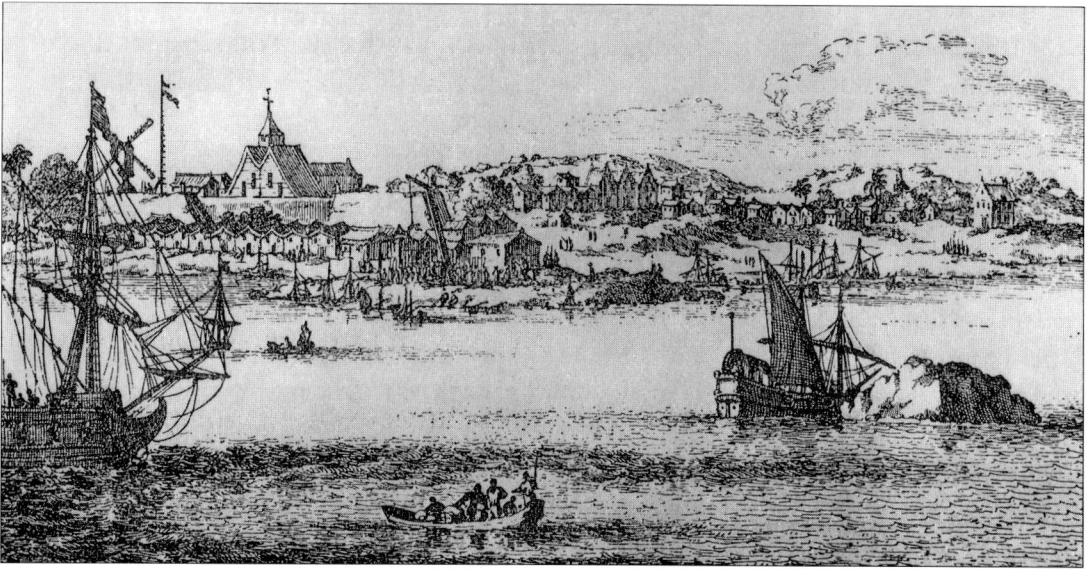

were hard. There was no difficulty finding customers, for a merchant who landed his cargo without paying tax was able to sell his goods more cheaply.

Wise laws?

In the countries of Europe, many people believed that colonies were set up for one reason alone: to help their mother country become rich. This idea was fiercely held in Britain. Here trade laws and taxes – such as the ones that the smugglers avoided – were part of the grand design. They were meant to make the colonies of America useful to Britain. Government officials in London spoke of their *'wise laws'* and devised more schemes to *'tie trade to the mother country'*.

Until the middle of the eighteenth century, many of these 'wise laws' were disobeyed. There was a great deal of smuggling and little was done to prevent it. From the year 1763 onwards, this began to change. Britain was worried about the cost of maintaining a growing empire. There had been expensive wars with the rival countries of France and Spain, and skirmishes with Native Americans to pay for. In a bid to raise money, Britain ordered its tax collectors in America to declare war on the smugglers. New trade laws and new

As the sea was an important highway in colonial times, many of the first American settlements were established on the coast. This is New Amsterdam, which was later renamed New York.

taxes were introduced to bring in more money. Sugar, coffee, wine and silks were some of the goods taxed by one new law. This was known as the Sugar Act, and it was passed in 1764. Other laws followed. In 1765 the Stamp Act placed a tax on all sorts of papers and documents, from news-papers to advertisements, and in 1773 the Tea Act made unpopular changes in the way that tea was to be paid for in America.

These laws brought violent reactions. Many people in America refused to buy tea. In Boston, Massachusetts, there was a dramatic protest against the Tea Act in 1773. Settlers disguised as Native Americans tipped a cargo of tea worth £15,000 into the harbour from ships waiting to unload. This event became known as the Boston 'Tea Party'.

All sorts of ingredients found in the kitchen were taxed, from tea to sugar and rum. British taxes became more and more unpopular during the 1760s and early 1770s.

Taxes and loyalty

In London, the government was convinced that its trade laws were just. In America, however, there were very different views. There was a growing feeling that trade and industry were being held back unfairly by British actions. This pushed some people into developing new and explosive ideas about politics. Some suggested that Britain had no right to make laws and taxes for America because the American people had no one to represent their view in Parliament in London. 'No taxation without representation' was their rallying cry. Extreme views like these were expressed by some American lawyers, such as James Otis (1725–1783) and Patrick Henry (1736–1799), and by some politicians, including Samuel Adams (1722–1803). Some of these men even began to ask whether they could continue to be loyal to the king, George III, when America was treated in this way. Questions like this were soon to bring revolutionary change.

THE REBEL

In 1775 war broke out between the American colonies and Britain. The Americans who fought against the British were known as rebels. Their cause was stated in a famous document called the Declaration of Independence, which was drafted by Thomas Jefferson of Virginia (1743–1826):

'We … declare that these united colonies are and of right ought to be free and independent states … All political connection between them and Great Britain is … totally dissolved.'

'I am an American'

A gap had grown between Britain and the colonies since the days of the Pilgrim Fathers in the 1620s. The first settlers had thought of themselves as people from Europe who lived in a foreign land. As time went by, their ties with the Old World grew weak. People became aware that they had a new identity: many no longer regarded themselves as British subjects but instead were loyal to the colony where they now lived. Some also began to realize that although each colony had its own distinct way of life, their inhabitants had more in common with each other than they had with the people of Europe. A lawyer from Philadelphia who was a strong supporter of the American side during the war with Britain summed up these feelings. His name was Patrick Henry. *'I am not a Virginian, but an American,'* he declared. Henry meant that his loyalty to America was more important than his loyalty to Virginia, the colony where he lived. The feeling that America was

A rebel soldier stands proudly in front of the American flag. But not all the settlers of the British colonies wanted independence. Those who supported Britain were sometimes called 'Loyalists' or 'Tories'.

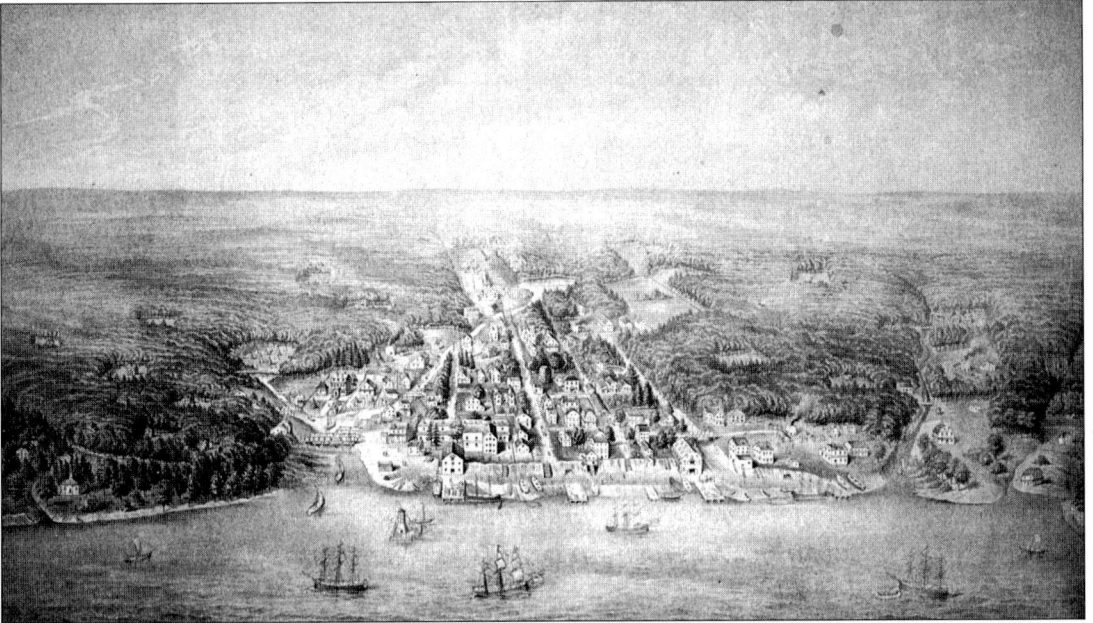

The town of Philadelphia in 1702. Philadelphia was fast growing into America's busiest town. It was home to many merchants and businessmen. One of these, a famous man named Benjamin Franklin, worked for the rebel side by trying to win support from France and other countries.

one nation, whose people should act together, was slow to develop but later became very important.

Thinking about politics

The people of America borrowed the ideas of thinkers in Britain and France to develop their own political arrangements. They took up the idea that all men were created equal, and that they had certain basic rights. This was a great challenge to the way society was organized in Europe. In Europe there was no question of equality; kings, queens and people from a noble background were treated as the most important members of society.

American politicians and lawyers also adopted the idea that only a government which treated the people in a good and fair manner had the right to expect to be obeyed. A government needed the people's consent. If it lost support by acting unjustly, it no longer had the right to rule.

These ideas made some people take a new look at the way Britain used its power over the American colonies. They asked if Britain had lost its right to

rule the colonies because it had made unfair laws and taxes.

Fighting for independence

To the government in Britain, American ideas about politics seemed threatening. There were no countries in Europe which tried to put ideas like these into practice. The clash of convictions led to war in 1775.

The American rebels were served by men such as Paul Revere, who became famous for his midnight ride from Boston to Concord in Massachusetts to warn the people that British troops were coming. The rebels were commanded by George Washington, who built up the army and became the first president after the war. There was work for politicians as well. The colonial structure of assemblies and governors remained, but it was adapted to suit new needs. And the title of 'colonies' was abandoned in favour of the proud name of 'states'. The states learned to take political decisions together. Joining together as 'united states', they met to create a 'congress' (parliamentary body) to speak for all the American people. Although some people did not want independence, in many places the war became a battle fought by the whole community. While men went to join the army, women turned to business and farming. One woman described how her grandmother worked in this way: *'She saw to every kind of business: the farm, the iron-works, and the family.'*

Thanks to efforts like these, America won its independence. By the end of the war in 1783, America had thrown off British control. It became the first 'republic' (a nation ruled without a king or queen) in modern history.

George Washington, commander of the rebel army. Having led America to victory in war, Washington was chosen to lead in peace time, too. He became the first president of the United States of America.

GLOSSARY

Apprentice A boy or girl training to take up a craft or other skill at work.

Assembly A meeting of men who decided how a colony should be ruled.

Blacksmith Someone who works with metal, especially iron.

Colony A place ruled by people from another land.

Constable An officer who helps keep law and order.

Convict A prisoner.

Craftsman Someone who makes things by hand.

Crime A deed that breaks the law.

Empire Colonies ruled by one country.

Goldsmith A craftsman who works with gold.

Goodwife The name given to a married woman in medieval Britain and colonial America.

Governor Someone who led the government of a colony.

Independent Free. Not ruled by another person or country.

Medicine man A Native American who was believed to have special powers with the spirit world. He was believed to be able to heal people who were ill because of these powers.

Mother country A country which sets up colonies in another land.

Native Americans People who lived in America when settlers from Europe arrived. The settlers called these people 'Indians'.

New World The name given to the Americas by the people of Europe.

Old World The name given to Europe.

Persecution A punishment given to someone because of his or her religious beliefs.

Pilgrim Fathers The group of settlers who sailed to Plymouth, New England, in a ship called the *Mayflower* in 1620. They likened their journey to a new land to a religious journey or pilgrimage.

Plantation A large farm.

Planter Someone who runs a plantation.

Proprietary colony A colony owned by one man, known as a proprietor. The proprietor had a great deal of power in the way that the colony was run.

Proprietor The owner of a colony.

Protestant A Christian who does not accept the teaching of the Pope, and who is not a member of the Roman Catholic Church.

Puritan A Protestant Christian with very strict beliefs and way of life.

Quaker A Christian who worships God in a simple way. The Quakers were greatly influenced by the ideas of a man called George Fox.

Roman Catholic A Christian who accepts the teaching of the Pope as the head of the Church.

Sabbath The Christian holy day and day of rest: Sunday.

Settlement A town or village built by people coming to live in a new place.

Settler Someone who goes to live in a new land.

Smuggler Someone who breaks the law by bringing goods into the country without paying tax.

Tax Money paid to the government.

Wampum belt A beaded belt made by Native Americans. The beads formed a kind of writing, so that information could be recorded on a wampum belt.

Wharf A place for a boat to tie up and land.

FURTHER READING

For Children

Clorinda Clarke, *American Revolution 1775–83*, Longman, 1964.

The People of the Past, The Seventeenth Century, OUP, 1967.

Glenys Ambrus, *The Pilgrim Fathers*, A & C Black, 1974.

For Adults

Richard Middleton, *Colonial America, A History (1607–1760)*, Blackwell, 1992.

Darrett B Rutman, *Winthrop's Boston, A Portrait of a Puritan Town 1630–1649*, W W Norton & Co, 1972.

Rhys Isaac, *The Transformation of Virginia 1740–1790*, W W Norton & Co, 1988.

Linda K Kerber, *Women of the Republic; Intellect and Ideology in Revolutionary America*, W W Norton & Co, 1986.